The Ultimate Golf Fitness Program

A 12-Week Workout Plan for Golfers

Brandon Gaydorus & Lauren McMillin

ISBN: 9798432238887

Disclaimer: The reader should be cautioned that there is an inherent risk assumed by the participant with any form of physical activity. Those participating in strength and conditioning programs should check with their physician prior to initiating such activities. Anyone participating in these activities should understand that such training initiatives may be dangerous if performed incorrectly. The authors assume no liability for injury; this was put together for educational purposes. It's important for participants to have full knowledge, understanding, and appreciation of the dangers involved with physical activity.

DEDICATION

For every golfer who has ever known the joy of the game. May this
program give you freedom through movement, both on and off the course.

CONTENTS

ACKNOWLEDGMENTS

From Lauren:

Thank you to the many teachers and mentors who have paved the way and led by example. Your influence has changed my life for the better, and I am eternally grateful for your guidance and encouragement.

To my parents – thank you for enthusiastically believing in me and supporting me every step of the way. And thank you to Gus, the true star of the show and my favorite little fluff. I love you the most.

From Brandon:

Thank you to all those who have supported, whether you were a mentor, family member, friend, client or business associate. A book like this would not be possible without you.

And a massive thank you to our videographer and photographer, Vin Mizzoni.

INTRODUCTION

Although golf fitness may be one of the industry's newer trends, if today's tour players are any indication, it won't be going away anytime soon.

Competitive golfers seem to spend an extensive amount of time in the gym with a specific focus, just like they do on the course.

Why?

Because becoming more physically fit can lead to longer drives, increased swing speed, fewer injuries, more endurance, a smoother turn, and a better transition through impact!

Sounds simple, right? Hit the gym, do some stretches, spend some time on a piece of cardio equipment, and you did what needed to be done.

That may help, but you'll likely quit from boredom or start to see a flatline in results, due to the repetitiveness of the program.

The problem with one-size-fits-all fitness programs is that golfers are all built differently, and have individual goals and needs. An instructor gives you a lesson or a tip, asking you to move in a specific way. But what if you aren't able to perform the movement properly?

It's the same thing when you're working on getting in shape. If you immediately start to hit the weights but don't have the mobility in your joints to safely build strength, you're setting yourself up for possible injuries in the future.

Our goal with the Ultimate Golf Fitness Program is to meet you at your current fitness level and give you an easy plan to follow.

There are two different tracks that you can choose from: **Stability** and **Strength**. Each program starts with mobility, as we believe proper mobility is the foundation to all movement.

We'll give you the tools and insights you need to both feel and perform your best. You'll also take a self-guided physical assessment to determine which program is optimal for you.

Working out can get very complicated, expensive, and boring.

So, we have designed this book to keep things as simple as possible, with a low cost and high return.

Keep in mind, if you were to go through these programs in private sessions throughout the 12 weeks with either of us, it would cost nearly $5,000.

Since we knew how valuable this could be for golfers all over the world, we wanted to create this affordable and effective alternative. Please understand though, that the tradeoff is that you will need to do some of the work on your own by studying the exercises beforehand, because we won't be with you to give immediate feedback.

If you have any questions, please email us and we will do our best to get back to you as soon as possible.

Lauren McMillin – lauren.m.mcmillin@gmail.com

Brandon Gaydorus – bgaydorus@gmail.com

PICKING THE RIGHT PROGRAM FOR YOU

Before selecting a program, let's begin with a self-guided physical assessment to see how your body moves in all three planes of motion.

Our entire mobility program is based on the movement of these three planes of motion, so we want you to have a better understanding of what they are and how each plane of motion relates to the golf swing.

The mobility program is the same for both the Stability and Strength tracks, as it's the foundation of all movements.

We designed the mobility program into three lower and three upper body movements that hit each plane of motion.

3 Planes of Motion [1]

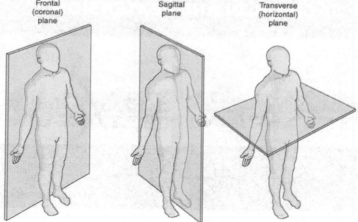

So now let's dive into the evaluation…

---

[1] Dtankov. "Core Stability with a Twist." Motus Sport & Spine, 29 Sept. 2017. https://motussportandspine.com/core-stability-twist/.

Sagittal Plane (Forward & Backward)

For the sagittal of motion, imagine a line separating the left and right halves of your body. When you bend forward (flexion) and backward (extension), you are moving along the sagittal plane.

In golf, you get in this plane by hinging from your hips, knees, and ankles when standing at address.

Additionally, at the top of the backswing, your lower back will be mostly in extension to help get more width and create a better turn, while it then flexes on the downswing to clear room for the hips throughout impact.

Sagittal Mobility Testing: From a standing position, place one foot forward while extending your arms overhead. Proceed to reach back as far as you can without losing your balance, then return to your starting position. Repeat 5-8 times on each side.

Then step one foot back into a lunge as shown on the image below, while sweeping your arms down and back. Let your spine round before returning to the starting position. Repeat 5-8 times on each side.

SAGITTAL PLANE - FLEXION

Stand with arms reaching at shoulder height, feet hip-width apart

Step one foot back, bending knees and rounding spine. Sweep arms down and behind. Repeat 5 times with each leg. To test stability, hover the lead foot.

golfmobilitypro.com

Sagittal Stability: Repeat the same movements, but try not to let your moving leg touch the floor. This indicates the stability in your standing leg, including the foot, ankle, knee and hip.

What You're Testing: These movements show you how well your ankles move while your feet stay grounded, as well as how your hips, t-spine (mid-back), and shoulders flex and extend.

Takeaways: If you find the stability part of this exercise hard to do, we'd recommend starting with the stability program for at least one phase.

Frontal Plane (Side-to-Side)

The frontal or lateral plane divides the body into front and back halves. Movements in this plane occur in the form of bending from side to side (laterally), as well as your limbs moving both toward (adduction) and away from (abduction) your center.

In golf, this happens when your hips sway or slide, when your shoulders dip in either direction, or when your arms extend away from your body.

Frontal Mobility: Stand with your arms overhead. Place your left foot across the midline of your body, then move it to the right as shown in the picture below. At the same time, reach your arms to the opposite side as you bend your torso. Return to the starting position and repeat 5-8 times on each side.

Frontal Stability: Repeat the same movements, but try not to let your moving leg touch the ground. This indicates the stability in your standing leg, including the foot, ankle, knee and hip, as well as strength in your torso, especially the obliques.

What You're Testing: These movements indicate how well your body moves through abduction and adduction, as well as lateral flexion in the spine.

During every golf swing your spine laterally flexes and tilts to the side. Without lateral flexion, you'll have a flat shoulder turn, making it more challenging to create a repeatable impact position.

With a lack of mobility or stability in your hip rotators, it will be tough to stay centered throughout the swing, leading to topped and thin shots that cause many golfers nightmares, because of too much swaying or sliding.

Takeaways: If you find yourself losing balance pretty easily while your leg is moving or off the ground, we'd recommend starting with the stability program for at least one phase.

Transverse Plane (Rotational)

Finally, it's important to examine the transverse plane, otherwise known as the rotational plane. This plane divides the body into upper and lower halves and is already familiar to most golfers, as it's heavily utilized throughout your swing.

Transverse Mobility: Stand with your arms extended in front of your body at shoulder-height. Step your right foot to the side, moving into a side lunge. Reach your arms to the right, turning your shoulders but keeping your gaze forward. Return to the starting position and repeat 5-8 times on each side.

Transverse Stability: Rather than stepping into a side lunge, lift your moving leg off the floor and practice turning your leg and torso to each side.

TRANSVERSE PLANE

✕ Stand on one leg with arms extended in front of you.

✕ Rotate torso and shoulders toward the standing leg. Keep gaze forward and back leg lifted. Unwind. Repeat 5 times with each leg.

golfmobilitypro.com

What You're Testing: These movements test mobility and stability in the transverse plane, which indicates your ability to turn your torso and rotate your hips. We're mainly looking for your body's ability to separate the upper from the lower, which directly correlates to maximizing your power potential throughout the swing.

Takeaways: If you find yourself losing balance while your leg is up, we'd recommend starting with the stability program for at least one phase.

THE TRAINING PYRAMID

Since the first part of each program is mobility, here's a brief introduction to what we actually mean by that…

By definition, mobility refers to "the range of motion through which an individual can move one or a group of joint complexes with the desired speed, precision, and resistance to both internal and external forces."[2] In other words, it's important to be able to move your joints through their full range of motion in order to stay healthy and maximize your swing potential.

Mobility is the foundational component of any form of movement, and it is especially critical for your golf swing. If your body does not have the proper mobility required to move through the force of a golf swing, you'll set yourself up for injury, muscular imbalances, and ultimately frustration.

Mobility vs Flexibility

Many people confuse mobility with flexibility. While you need both, they are fundamentally different concepts.

Flexibility refers to the length of your muscle fibers, as well as your ability to stretch and move on a myofascial level. Myofascia is the connective tissue that spans across the entire body and is often the culprit of "tight muscles."

On the other hand, mobility is directly related to the range of motion in your joints. Beyond that, mobility includes control. While you need to move your joints to the extent that they are designed, you also need to control

---

[2] Davies, C., & DiSaia, V. (2019). *Golf Anatomy* (p. 35). Human Kinetics.

that movement with stability and balance.

A simple illustration of this happens in the golf swing when you move through the downswing and transition into the follow-through.

You must decelerate your swing and control how you finish. Without this, your body would continue to spin around, and you would lose all control over it.

So, when thinking about mobility, think beyond flexibility and range of motion. Remember that it involves both movement and resistance to movement.

The Goal of the Warm-Up

Now that you know the planes of motion the body moves in and that mobility is the foundation of all movement, it's important to understand what the goal of the warm-up actually is.

"Warm-up" is a broad and general term that is often skipped or looked over, compared to the intense part of a workout. We get it; it's typically not as fun, and may even feel like a waste of time! But if done properly, it actually saves you recovery time, and will help you get more out of your workout.

Here are the four main goals of a warm-up, to prepare both the body and mind appropriately for increased effectiveness, and to help avoid injury on and off the course.

1) Prime the Mobility You Already Have

Just like you brush your teeth every day to keep them looking and feeling good, it's important to do the same thing with your joints by moving them well and often. Examples of mobile joints include the ankle, hips, torso, shoulders and neck.

2) Prepare the Central Nervous System (CNS)

The CNS is made up of the brain and spinal cord.

The brain is an organ made up of nervous tissue, which pioneers the actions and thoughts of the human body, while the spinal cord relays information from the rest of the body to the brain.

With proper movement and coordination exercises built into the warm-up, the central nervous system will be prepared efficiently.[3]

3) Increase Tissue Temperature

If the goal of the warm-up is to warm you up, then it's essential to focus on increasing the tissue temperature of the body. In return, the body is able to absorb and adapt more efficiently to the stress of the workout and/or golf round.

4) Get You Ready for the Specific Task at Hand

People often wonder about the best exercise to do before a round of golf.

Our answer is always going to be to hit balls before you play. Swinging a club is the most specific exercise to the game, and it prepares the body for the round ahead.

Stability Program

This program, combined with the mobility warm-up, should take about 30-40 minutes. You'll have two different routines that can be repeated up to four days a week. You'll have six exercises to do in each routine, including three upper and three lower body movements for each plane of motion (sagittal, frontal, transverse). We recommend going through these exercises three times, but you can do one or two rounds depending on the level of difficulty.

Although we believe this program works for most golfers, it's challenging to have a general program that works for everyone. Use your best judgment if something doesn't feel right. For example, we do a lot of kneeling positions in Phase 1 to help build the foundational elements of stability in your ankles, knees and hips. If you have difficulty with the kneeling positions, please email us or check with your local personal trainer for exercise alternatives.

Strength Program

This program, combined with the mobility warm-up, should take about 40-55 minutes. This also consists of two separate routines, which can be

---

[3] Haff, G., Triplett, T. (2016). *ESSENTIALS of STRENGTH TRAINING and CONDITIONING: Forth Edition*, 8-9. Human Kinetics.

repeated for up to four days a week.

Days 1 & 3 focus mostly on the front of your body through various knee-dominant (Ex. Squats) and upper body pressing (Ex. Dumbbell Bench Press) exercises. Additionally, the warm-up circuit focuses on power, core and hip activation exercises in the sagittal plane.

Days 2 & 4 will focus mostly on the back of your body through various hip-dominant (Ex. Glute Bridges & Deadlift Variations) and upper body pulling (Ex. Dumbbell Row) exercises. Additionally, the warm-up circuit focuses on power, core and hip activation exercises in the frontal and transverse planes.

FAQ's

What equipment do you need?

For both programs you'll need a yoga mat or pillow, golf club, and mini-band at minimum. Dumbbells, a weight bench, and if possible, a cable cross machine are also highly recommended for the Strength program. We have actually designed a home golf fitness package through Super Flex Fitness, which can be purchased at https://www.superflexfitness.com/shop/home-golf-fitness-home-package/.

How long is each phase?

There are three 4-week phases for both programs.

Phase 1: Weeks 1-4
Phase 2: Weeks 5-8
Phase 3: Weeks 9-12

What are your thoughts on barefoot training?

We believe shoes are important, but that adding more barefoot time in your days will pay dividends for you on and off the course.

How do I choose the right amount of weight to use?

Use your best judgment. Don't be afraid to start light and work your way up. We recommend increasing weight throughout the set. For example, if you're doing dumbbell bench presses and want to end at 55 pounds, and you have three sets, maybe go 45 for the 1st, 50 for the 2nd, and 55 for the

3rd.

What warm-up should I do before golf?

The mobility warm-up can be done before you play, but if you want to increase power from your warm-up and you have a solid base level of strength, we recommend *The Ultimate Golf Fitness Warm-Up* which can be found on our Golf Mobility Pro YouTube Channel.

Are these workouts designed to help avoid injuries?

Yes, we place a major emphasis on injury prevention, because it's common for golfers of all levels to experience aches and pains over the course of their playing career.

Should I do breath work?

While there is some breathing work incorporated with the exercises, we did not make it a priority for this book. For additional breathing exercises, you can check out Season 2, Episode 4 *Post Round Recovery* from our YouTube show, Golf Mobility Pro.

How do I use the door attachment in the Home Golf Fitness Package?

Door attachments can look a little confusing at first, but they're really pretty simple.

The side you're pulling from should be opposite of the door hinges. All you do from there is slip one side through the crack between the door and the doorframe, then shut the door.

Pull on it to make sure it's nice and sturdy. Then place the band around the door attachment.

If some of the exercises don't work for me, are there alternatives?

Absolutely! For exercises that may utilize different levels of equipment, we offer variations. If you have questions about certain exercises, we encourage you to reach out to us. We are happy to provide clarification, offer video help, or suggest alternative exercises.

How do I know which program to follow?

Great question! If you have little training experience and equipment, we'd recommend the stability program. It usually takes about 30-40 minutes to complete.

If you want to do strength training, it has options for both limited equipment and full access to a gym. There is also a "no jump protocol" if your body isn't prepared to jump. This program typically takes 40-55 minutes.

What if I have limited space?

We took a lot of time developing programs that people could do with limited space and equipment. With our stability and strength programs, you can do exactly that.

PHASE 1: MOBILITY (ALL LEVELS – 1 ROUND)

Hamstring Floss

Place both hands behind your leg as shown. Bring your knee toward your face, bending the back of your knee to a 90-degree angle.

Keep your ankle flexed and bottom leg straight.

From there, extend the lower leg up into a vertical position, then back down to a 90-degree angle. Perform 8 times, then repeat with the other leg.

Keep The Ankles Flexed

Supine Hip External Rotations

Lying on the ground, place one of your ankles on the top of the outside of the other leg's knee.

Grab the outside of the knee with one hand and the shin with the other.

Then pull toward your chest, putting more tension on the knee than the shin. You should feel this on the outside hip (glute area) of the leg you're pulling toward your chest. Hold for 15 seconds, then repeat with the other leg.

Supine Side-to-Side Leg Sweeps

Lying on your back in a relaxed position, lift one leg about a foot off the ground.

From there, keep your leg straight and sweep it to the side, and then reverse it the other way. Perform 8 times, then repeat with the other leg.

If this puts strain on your lower back, try placing a band around your foot to make it a bit easier. While the lower back may come off the ground slightly, try to keep it connected to the floor.

Supine Pelvic Tilts

Lying on your back, place one hand on your stomach and the other on your chest.

Keeping your feet flat on the ground with your knees bent, take a deep breath in, expanding through the stomach and chest.

Your lower back will slowly start to lift and arch. As you exhale, press your lower back into the ground. Perform 8 times.

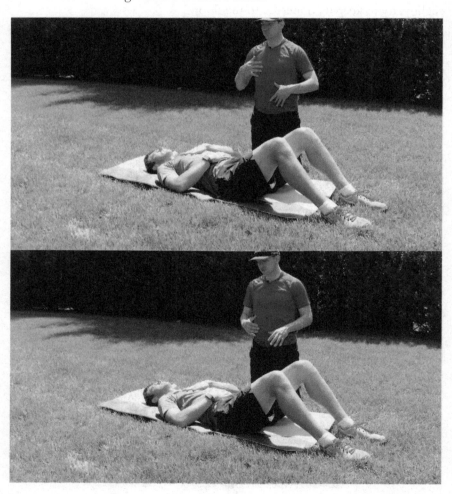

Side-Lying Open Books

Lie on your side and use your bottom arm as a pillow for your head.

Place your top leg out in front of you as pictured. This helps to secure your lower body from moving throughout the exercise.

From there, arc your top arm backwards toward the ground, opening your chest. Try to keep your elbow above shoulder-height. The hand does not need to touch the ground. Focus on keeping the lower body still. Perform 8 times, then repeat on the other side of your body.

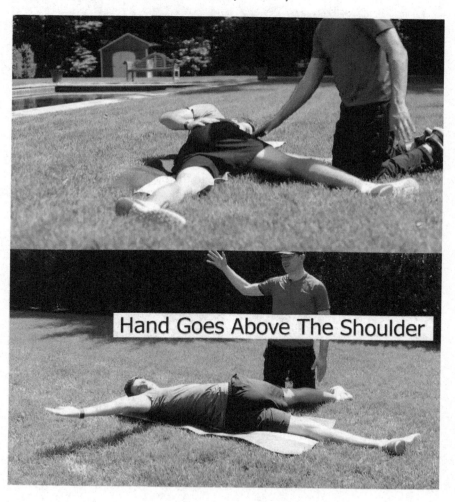

Hand Goes Above The Shoulder

Half-Kneeling Quad Pull with Overhead Reach

Start from a half-kneeling position, one knee on the ground and the other in front of you, both at a 90-degree angle. (If you're kneeling on a hard surface, feel free to place a cushion beneath your knee.)

Lean forward until you feel a nice stretch in the back leg.

Once you feel the stretch, raise up the arm opposite of the forward knee.

Then tilt inward and reach up until feeling a nice stretch along that side of your body. Hold for 15 seconds, then repeat on the other side.

For a more challenging version, place your back foot on an elevated surface. Press your hips forward, keeping your front heel down. To deepen the stretch, reach your arm up and side-bend away from the stretched leg.

Alternative Exercise: Child's Pose

If the half-kneeling quad pull is uncomfortable, you can do the child's pose instead.

For this exercise, start on your hands and knees.

Then reach your arms forward while moving your hips toward your heels. If you can't get your hips all the way to your heels, place a cushion or foam roller between your knees and calves to add some support. Hold for 15 seconds.

PHASE 2: MOBILITY (ALL LEVELS – 1 ROUND)

Assisted Leg Lowers

Place a resistance band around the middle of your foot and grab onto each side of the band.

Extend the leg with the band around it and try to keep it as straight as possible.

Raise the opposite leg up and down under a controlled movement. Perform 5 times, then repeat with the other leg.

You can also perform this without the band if you have solid hamstring mobility, meaning your leg is fairly straight and there's about a 90-degree angle between the legs from the starting position.

90/90 Hip Internal + External Rotation

In a seated position, bend the knees as shown, with feet wider than your hips.

Start by dipping your knees to the right while keeping a 90-degree angle between the back of both knees.

Then bend your torso to your right, bring your left arm across your body and through the space beneath your right arm.

Lift your left knee up as far as you can while keeping the right knee down. When you can't go any further, rotate both knees to the other side. Perform 5 times, alternating from side to side.

To increase the level of difficulty, place your hands to the side and repeat the same movement.

Half-Kneeling Adductor Walkout

Place one leg straight and out to the side as pictured below. The inside of that foot should be flat on the ground.

Rock backwards and walk the hands back, before then walking forward and dropping your hips toward the ground. Make sure to keep the spine neutral and away from too much extension. Perform 5 times, then repeat on the other side of your body.

Cat & Camel

On your hands and knees (quadruped position). Make sure your shoulders are directly over your wrists, and your hips over your knees. Push your lower spine toward the ground while pulling your chin up toward the sky.

Then reverse this movement by tucking the neck downward and letting the mid-lower part of the spine follow upward. Keep the arms straight the entire time. Perform 5 times in each position, slowly rotating between the two.

If you feel pressure on your knees, kneel on a cushion.

Quadruped T-Spine External Rotations

Kneel on the ground, placing your knees together. Put one hand behind your head.

From there, rotate that arm's elbow toward the sky, retracting your shoulder back as you do. Keep the opposing forearm on the ground, and push your hips toward your heels (use a foam roller to bridge the gap if needed).

Once you get to the top, hold for a second, then bring the elbow back to the ground. Perform 5 times, then repeat on the other side of your body.

Seated Lateral Tilts or Tall-Kneeling Lateral Flexion

Choose whichever exercise suits you best.

For the seated lateral tilts, sit on a chair or bench and bring your knees together.

Place your hands behind your head, keeping your elbows wide.

Keep your lower body still and knees close together as you turn your upper body to the right. Dip your trail shoulder down, crunching the right obliques. Return to the center and repeat to the left. Perform 5 times on each side.

For the tall-kneeling lateral flexion, place your hands behind your head and sit back onto your heels.

Rotate as far as you can and tilt downward, as shown in the pictures. Try to not let your chest fall forward as you do this exercise.

Repeat on the other side, alternating for the prescribed amount. Perform 5 times for each side.

PHASE 3: MOBILITY (ALL LEVELS – 1 ROUND)

Toe Touches (Toes Up + Heels Up)

Place your toes on a slightly elevated surface about two inches off of the ground.

Extend your hips forwards, reach up, and breathe in.

Hold for a second, then breathe out and curl your spine downwards, starting from the neck down to the lower back.

If your hamstrings or lower back are tight, perform this movement with knees bent.

After this, elevate your heels and repeat the same process. Stand with the heels slightly elevated. On an inhale, reach your arms overhead. As you exhale, reach your arms toward the floor, letting your body fold inward. Perform 5 times each way.

Standing Hip Twists

Place one leg on an object such as a bench, box or chair. The leg should stay straight and be at about knee- to hip-height.

If you're new to this exercise or struggle with balance, make sure your hand is near something to hold.

From there, twist your hips inward and outward as shown below. Make sure the leg on the ground stays straight and that the foot stays facing forward. Perform 8 times with each leg.

Leg Swings

Place your hands on something sturdy and swing the moving leg side to side.

Open the foot as you swing away from the body and then turn in when coming inward with the other leg. Perform 15 times with each leg.

Pelvic Tilts

Get into a golf stance and place your hands across your chest or on the side of your hips.

From there, tuck your pelvis in and out. Try to keep the separation smooth and under control. Perform 8 times in each direction.

Placing the hands on the hips (pictured below) can help initiate this separation, especially when first starting out.

Torso Rotations

Get into a golf stance and place your hands across your chest.

From there, keep your lower body still and alternate the rotation of your upper body.

Make sure the downward-tilted shoulder points toward the ground. Perform 8 times for each direction.

Lateral Line Stretch

Stand with your golf club overhead (can also perform without one) and place your hands slightly wider than your shoulders.

Tap one foot across your body, leaning your upper body the opposite way.

Hold for 15 seconds, then return to the starting position and perform on the other side.

STABILITY WORKOUT – PHASE 1 (Day 1 & 3)

Perform in Order for 3 Rounds Each

Glute Bridge Holds

Lying on your back, bend your knees and place your feet flat on the ground.

Lower your arms by your sides and keep the palms down.

Press your feet into the floor as you lift your hips. Avoid letting your legs cave in, and make sure to maintain space between your chest and your chin. Hold for 30 seconds.

Iso-Split Squat Hold with Twist (Alternative: Half-Kneeling)

Start from a half-kneeling position with the knees at 90-degree angles as shown below. Then lift the back knee off the ground and hover it a few inches off the floor.

Hold a golf club in front of you at shoulder-height and twist your upper body toward the side of the forward foot. Perform 8 times on each side of your body.

If it is too difficult to do with the knee lifted, keep it down and perform the rotational component of the exercise.

Side-Lying Abductions

Lying on your side, rest your top foot on an elevated object. Then lift up and hold for 10 seconds, 2 times for each leg.

Avoid letting the top foot point upward. You should feel this on the outside of your top leg.

Push-Up Holds or Plank from Hands and Knees

For the push-up holds, stack your shoulders over your wrists and extend your legs behind you, so that your body is in a straight line. Hold for 20 seconds.

For the plank from hands and knees, place your elbows directly below your shoulders and rest your knees on the ground. It should feel like the elbows are sliding toward the knees. Hold for 20 seconds.

Half-Kneeling Golf Club Chop/Lift

From a half-kneeling position, grip a golf club as if you were driving a motorcycle.

Proceed to sweep the golf club down before lifting it up as you turn over the front leg. Start slow and, if your balance is stable, pick-up speed as you go. Perform 8 times for each leg.

Side Plank from Knees

Place your elbow directly below your shoulder while stacking your knees on top of each other.

Then lift up your hips, making sure that your knees are in front of your body and that your feet are behind your glutes as shown in the pictures. Hold for 5 seconds a total of 5 times, then repeat on the other side of your body.

You should feel this on the side of your core. The upper body should stay perpendicular to the floor throughout the exercise.

Alternative: Star Planks

If the side plank from knees is too challenging or bothers your shoulder, you can do a star plank.

Attach a band to something sturdy and keep your body upright as you lift your outside foot up. Hold for 25 seconds, then repeat with your other foot.

STABILITY WORKOUT – PHASE 1 (Day 2 & 4)

Perform in Order for 3 Rounds Each

Full Ankle Dorsiflexion Split Squats

From the split stance position, place your lead foot on an elevated object about 3-6 inches off of the ground, and hold on to something sturdy.

Then lower the back knee toward the ground and drive the lead knee as far forward as you can, while keeping the heel of the front foot on the ground. Repeat this up-and-down motion 8 times, then repeat with the other leg.

Alternative: Half-Kneeling Knee Drives

From a half-kneeling position, elevate your front foot on a low surface as shown in the pictures.

Drive your lead knee forward while keeping your front heel down. Try to get your front knee to go over your toes. Return to the starting position and repeat 8 times, then repeat with the other leg.

Single Leg Balance

Stand on one leg and get into a golf posture.

Keep a slight bend in your knee and hold for 15 seconds. Repeat with the other leg.

To make this more challenging, close your eyes.

If it's difficult to maintain balance, then place your back toes softly on the ground for added stability.

Glute Max Press-Out

Lie on your side, stacking your hips and knees at a 90-degree angle. Use a foam roller or slightly elevated surface under your feet for increased activation.

With a fairly strong mini-band around the knees, lift the band up and hold for 5 seconds. Make sure the insides of the feet stay together as you lift up. Perform 5 times, then repeat on the other side of your body.

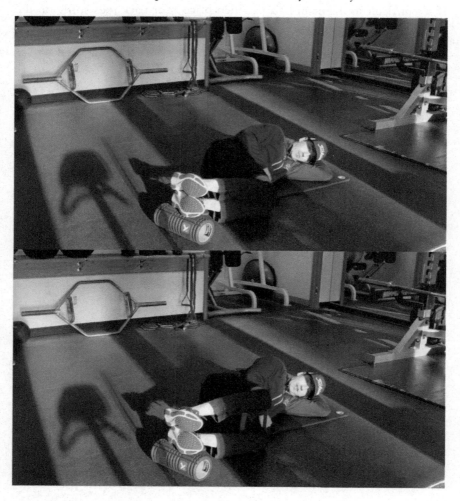

Supine Hip Drops

Lie on your back and hold a golf club above your shoulders. Proceed with this exercise by lifting your feet off the floor. Keep the knees at a 90-degree angle.

Start with the knees directly above the hips before lowering one leg at a time toward the ground. Perform 8 times, then change the order of the leg drops and repeat another 8 times.

Try to keep the lower back touching the ground throughout this exercise for increased core activation.

Tall-Kneeling Golf Swings

Kneeling on both knees, hold a golf club out in front of you.

The lower body will stay fairly still from this position. Simply swing as hard as you can 3 times. Repeat on both your dominant and non-dominant sides.

If this bothers your knees, perform it from the standing position or use some extra cushion, as a yoga mat may not be enough.

You can use a golf club or speed stick for this exercise; just try not to hit the ground when you swing.

90/90 Isometric Holds

Stand with feet about hip-width apart.

Hold your arms in a goal-post position, with the elbows bent at 90 degrees.

Retract your shoulders back and resist any movements in the arms. Hold in the three positions for 10 seconds apiece: palms facing the ears; thumbs close to the ears; palms away from the ears.

STABILITY WORKOUT – PHASE 2 (Day 1 & 3)

Perform in Order for 3 Rounds Each

Single Leg Glute Bridge Holds

Lie on your back and place your feet parallel to the floor. Then press one foot into the ground and bend the other knee toward your chest, forming a 90-degree angle. Maintaining this position, lift your hips off the ground. Hold for 10 seconds a total of 3 times, then repeat with the other leg.

Quarter Squat with Rotation

From a standing position, place one foot on an elevated surface about 3-6 inches off the ground.

Perform a quarter squat with the top leg while tapping the opposing heel toward the ground.

With your arms across your chest and lower body still, turn your upper body as shown in the second picture. Repeat 8 times, then repeat with the other leg. Make sure to keep most of your weight on the elevated leg.

Side-Lying Adduction Off Bench

Lie on your side and place your top leg on an elevated surface. Keep the top leg straight and bring your bottom foot to the inside of the top knee.

Using your adductors, or inner thigh muscles, lift your bottom knee off of the ground. Hold for 2 seconds a total of 8 times, then repeat on the other side.

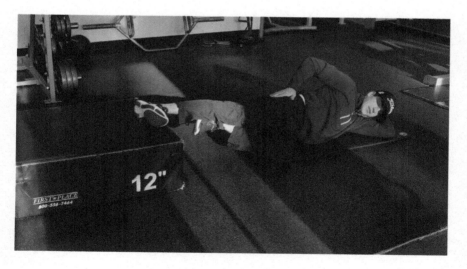

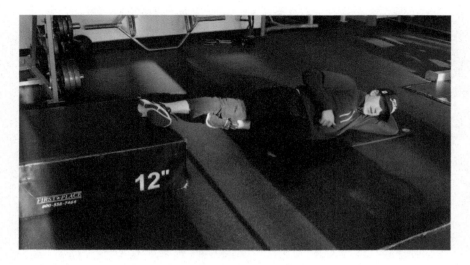

Split Stance Chop/Lift

From a split stance position, grip a golf club as if you were driving a motorcycle, with your knuckles on the top side.

Keep your lower body stable while lifting the club up and across your body. Make sure your arms are straight. Perform 8 times, then repeat in the opposite direction.

Side Plank from Knees with Abduction

Place your elbow directly below your shoulder while stacking your knees on top of each other.

Then lift your hips up, making sure your knees are in front of your body and your feet are behind your glutes as shown in the pictures. Once in position, lift the top knee and foot up and hold for 5 seconds, a total of 5 times. Repeat with the other leg.

You should feel this on the side of your core and outside of the legs. Your upper body should stay perpendicular to the floor throughout the exercise.

STABILITY WORKOUT – PHASE 2 (Day 2 & 4)

Perform in Order for 3 Rounds Each

Split Squat Holds

From a half-kneeling position, lift your back knee a couple of inches off the ground and hold for 5 seconds. Lower the knee and repeat 5 times, then repeat with the other leg.

If you feel pressure beneath your knees, kneel on a cushion.

Single Leg Balance with Alternating Reach

From a standing position, shift your weight to one leg and keep a slight bend in the standing leg.

Holding your balance, reach one arm across your body and alternate sides 8 times, then repeat in the opposite direction.

If it's too tough to maintain your balance, place your back toes lightly on the ground.

Glute Max Mini-Band Circuit

Place a strong mini-band just above your knees and get into a golf posture.

With your feet hip-width apart, keep one leg still and move the opposing leg in and out 8 times. Repeat on the other side.

Next, go in and out with the knees at the same time for another 8 times, and finish it by pressing the band out for 10 seconds.

Supine Dead Bug with Golf Club

Lying on your back, hold a golf club above your shoulders and lift your feet off the floor while keeping a 90-degree angle between the back of the knees, as pictured below.

Keep your back flat on the ground as you straighten one leg and rotate the opposing arm toward the inside of the bent knee. Perform 6 times, then repeat with the other leg.

Make sure the ankle stays flexed as you extend the leg out and to pull everything back to the starting position.

If this is too challenging or bothers the lower back, keep the knee bent or don't lower the leg as far.

Standing Swings

From a golf stance, swing the golf club as fast as you can with both your dominant and non-dominant sides, 5 times on each side.

Avoid hitting the ground as you swing. If you have access to a speed stick, we'd recommend using that instead of a club.

Tom House Push-Pulls

Place your forearms parallel to the floor and pull your hands apart. Hold for 15 seconds, then reverse the grip and repeat.

For the pushes, do the same thing except press the palms of the hands together as pictured. Only perform the exercise one way in this position.

The pulls should cause you to feel tension and activation in the back of the shoulder blades. The pushes should cause you to feel the front and outside areas of the pectoral muscles activate.

STABILITY WORKOUT – PHASE 3 (Day 1 & 3)

Perform in Order for 3 Rounds Each

Single Leg Glute Bridge

Lie on your back and place your feet flat on the ground. Lower your arms by your sides and keep the palms down.

Proceed to bring one knee toward your chest and press the opposite foot into the floor as you lift your hips. Perform this motion up and down 8 times, then repeat with the other leg.

You should feel this exercise in the back of the leg that is pushing into the ground.

Iso-Single Leg Deadlift with Twists

Stand on one leg and lift the other leg behind you. Lean forward slightly, keeping a neutral spine.

Then extend your arms out in front of you before opening them up. Rotate from side to side while keeping the lower body still. Perform 5 times, then repeat with the other leg.

If you are a little off-balance with this exercise, keep your back foot lightly on the ground throughout the movement.

Side-Lying Adduction Off Bench with Lift

Lying on your side, elevate your top leg on a plyo box or similar surface. Proceed to lift your bottom heel to the inside of the top knee using your adductors, or inner thigh muscles.

Keep the body perpendicular to the ground. Then press the inside of your foot into the box as you lift your hip off the ground. Hold for 5 seconds a total of 3 times, then repeat on the other side of your body. Avoid lifting the hip up if this is too challenging or you feel the onset of pain.

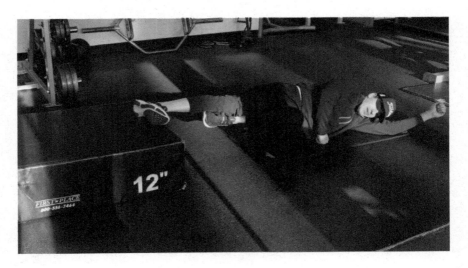

Shoulder Taps

Start in a push-up position, with the shoulders directly above the wrists.

Keep the rest of your body still and reach one hand across to tap the opposite shoulder. Release and repeat with the other hand. Perform 5 times in each direction, then add one additional rep each week.

To make this easier, keep your knees down throughout the movement or spread your feet out wider.

Lateral Lunge with Twist

Stand with a golf club held in front of you at shoulder-height. Your hands should be slightly wider than your shoulders, with the knuckles pointed up to the sky.

Start this movement by stepping to the side and bending the lead leg into a side lunge. Once in the bottom position, keep your lower body still and rotate the club and shoulders over the lead leg. Step back to your starting position and repeat on the other side. Repeat 5 times for each leg.

Side Plank

Place your feet on top of each other, or the top foot in front.

Make sure your shoulder is directly above your elbow. Then press the feet and forearm into the ground as you lift the hips up.

Perform this for a total of 8 times with a slight pause at the top, then repeat on the other side of your body. You should feel this exercise in the oblique muscles.

<u>STABILITY WORKOUT – PHASE 3 (Day 2 & 4)</u>

Perform in Order for 3 Rounds Each

Single Leg Split Squat

From a split stance position, bend the back knee toward the ground, forming two 90-degree angles for both knees. Before the knee touches, reverse the direction and extend the back knee up to the starting position.

Keep the heel of the front foot down the entire time and push up using both feet. Perform on one side 8 times, then switch.

Single Leg Balance with Rotation

Stand on one leg, with a slight bend in the knee on the ground, and another slight bend with the hips. Then lift the other leg behind you a touch off of the ground.

Keep your spine in a straight line and lower body still, before then turning your shoulders and torso from side to side. Perform this exercise 8 times on both sides.

Place the back foot slightly on the ground if you are struggling to maintain your balance.

Stiff Leg Lateral Walks

Stand with feet hip-width apart and place a light resistance band around your foot. Step-walk to the right 8 times, then step-walk to the left another 8 times.

Make sure to keep the legs straight and feet facing forward the entire time to get the most out of this exercise.

Extended Dead Bugs

Lying on your back, bend your knees to a 90-degree angle as pictured below. Reach your arms up over your shoulders before then lowering your right arm overhead and extending your left leg toward the ground to a slight hover. Return to the starting position and repeat on the other side. Perform 6 times on each side.

If this is too much for the lower back to handle, keep the knees bent throughout the movement.

Stepping Swings

From a golf stance, take a normal backswing. Then lift the front foot up and take a small step forward as you transition into the downswing. Swing as hard as you can. Use a speed stick if you have the option to.

Do this on both your dominant and non-dominant sides 5 times apiece.

Brandon Gaydorus & Lauren McMillin

Tom House Arm Circles

Place your shoulders back with elbows slightly bent.

Perform smooth and controlled small arm circles forward and backward for 10 seconds. Follow this with medium arm circles for 10 seconds, then large arm circles for 10 seconds.

With each round, switch the hand position to hit the shoulder a little bit differently each time, first palms down, then thumbs up, and finally palms up.

WARM-UP CIRCUIT – PHASE 1 (Days 1 & 3)

Perform in Order for 2 Rounds Each

Push-Up Hold or Plank from Knees

For the push-up hold, place your shoulders directly above your wrists. It should feel like your hands are twisting away from you.

Maintaining a neutral spine angle and straight arms, tense your glutes as if you were cracking a walnut between them, while tensing up your core as if you were to take a punch to the abdominal area. Hold for 20 seconds.

If the push-up hold bothers your wrists, perform the plank from your hands and knees.

The key to this exercise is to feel like your elbows are sliding toward your knees. This will help create the proper tension in the core.

Single Leg Hip Lift Holds

Lie on your back, flex your ankles toward your chest, and dig one heel into the ground.

From there, drive the opposing leg toward your chest as though you have a tennis ball between the hip and lower abdominals. Pretend as if you need to hold it there throughout the exercise.

Next, simply lift the hip and hold for 10 seconds. Perform 3 times, then repeat with the other leg.

Try to maintain a straight line from the shoulders to knee at the top position, as shown in the picture on the next page.

If you feel tension in your back, instead perform the hip lift with two feet.

Keep Both Ankles Flexed

Alternative: Hip Lift

The main goal with this exercise is to feel like you're tucking your hips as you lift, and like you're cracking a walnut between your glutes at the top position, to create the proper tension in your glutes and core.

Dead Bugs

Keep your back flat and spine neutral throughout the exercise.

Start by raising a golf club upward above shoulder-height.

Next, drive your knees toward your chest so that each display a 90-degree angle.

Keep one leg in place while lowering the other toward the ground. Lower the leg as far as you can without feeling tension in your lower back. Perform 8 times, then repeat with the other leg.

It's important to note that your ankles should stay flexed throughout the entire exercise.

For a more advanced version, turn the golf club inward toward the lowering leg, as shown in the pictures. Please note that this is not a big movement.

The rotation in the upper body helps to increase core tension.

Alternative: Supine Hip Drops

If the dead bugs produce pain in your lower back, then perform hip drops instead. Everything remains the same, except you keep the knee at a 90-degree angle as you lower the leg toward the ground.

Once the heel taps the ground softly, bring it back up and repeat with the other side.

Tall-Kneeling Chest Press

From a tall-kneeling position, attach the bands to something sturdy just above shoulder-height.

Once the bands are attached and on firmly, press the bands outward horizontally. Repeat 8 times.

Start slow, then pick up speed as you go. Keep the return motion under control.

Deceleration Jumps + Jumps

Perform five deceleration jumps by lifting up on the toes and reaching the hands up to the sky.

Next, reach the hands back as fast as you can as you load to the bottom position of a jump. Perform 5 times.

Next, perform five acceleration jumps by repeating the same movement as above, except jump upward after. Make sure to be explosive with this and to land softly.

<u>WARM-UP CIRCUIT – PHASE 1 (Day 2 & 4)</u>

Perform in Order for 2 Rounds Each

Side Plank from Knees with Abduction

Place your elbow directly below your shoulder, and knees stacked on top of each other.

Before lifting up, make sure the knees are in front of the hips and the feet behind them shown in the pictures.

Then lift the hips up and abduct the top leg up toward the sky. Hold for 5 seconds. Perform 5 times, then repeat on the other side of the body.

You should feel this on the side of the top leg and maybe a little on the bottom leg.

Alternating Lateral Lunge

Get into a wide stance and point your feet forward.

From there, lunge sideways into one leg and feel like you are loading the glute.

Alternate sides, repeating 5 times for each. Keep the knees facing forward the entire time.

Single Leg Balance with Eyes Closed

From a golf stance, shift onto one side so that you are balancing on one leg.

Once you are balanced, close your eyes for 15 seconds, then repeat on the other leg. If this is too difficult, keep the eyes open.

Half-Kneeling Rotational Band Throw

Attach a band about hip-height to a sturdy object, and place the inside knee down.

Grip the handle with the inside hand and overlap with the outside.

It should feel like you're throwing a medicine ball over your thigh. Control the movement on the way back in. Perform 8 times, then repeat on the other side of your body.

Start slow, and pick up speed as you go.

Lateral Bounds with Stick

Load into one leg and place that same arm behind you.

Jump as high and far as you can to the side, kind of like in the shape of a rainbow.

Stick the landing softly, then repeat in the other direction. Perform 5 times apiece.

<u>STRENGTH – PHASE 1 (Circuit 1 – Days 1 & 3)</u>

Perform in Order for 3 Rounds Each

<u>Oscillating Goblet Squat</u>
Weeks 1-4: 12 Reps

This exercise can be performed with a dumbbell, kettlebell, random weighted object, or your body weight.

Place the weight against your chest as shown in the pictures, and squat down to the bottom position with your thighs parallel to the floor.

If you can't get to that position, perform this exercise without a weight.

The oscillating part of this movement is to go halfway up from the bottom position and then right back down. You never go all the way up during this pulsing movement.

Half-Kneeling Overhead Press
Week 1: 12 Reps / Week 2-3: 10 Reps / Week 4: 8 Reps Each Side

Place a cable or resistance band somewhere sturdy below knee-height.

From there, press upward at about a 45-60 degree angle.

Try to keep the shoulder movement smooth and under control.

Extend At A 45-60 Degree Angle

Half-Kneeling Chop
Week 1: 8 Reps / Week 2-3: 10 Reps / Week 4: 12 Reps Each Side

Place a cable or resistance band about shoulder- to head-height on something sturdy.

Grip the band as if you were driving a motorcycle, with your knuckles pointed toward the sky. This is a core exercise, so try not to use just the arms as you chop down toward the bottom pocket of the outside leg.

Perform this movement under control with a tight core.

<u>STRENGTH – PHASE 1 (Circuit 2 – Days 1 & 3)</u>

Perform in Order for 3 Rounds Each

<u>Rear Foot Elevated (RFE) Split Squats</u>
Weeks 1-4: 5 (5 – Second Holds) Each Side

Use a low surface to elevate your back foot, similar to the height shown in the picture.

Bend until your other knee is at a 90-degree angle. Hold for five seconds at the bottom position, then explode up!

Make sure the front foot stays flat on the ground.

Depending on your level of strength, perform this using body weight or dumbbells.

<u>Alternative: Body Weight Split Squat</u>

If the previous exercise is too difficult with the foot elevated, perform it from the split squat position instead.

The lead knee should be just ahead of the front ankle, and the back toes dug into the ground.

Lift the front knee just off the ground and hold for five seconds.

Explode up and repeat.

Half-Kneeling Chest Press-Out or Single Arm Floor Press
Week 1: 12 Reps / Week 2-3: 10 Reps / Week 4: 8 Reps Each Side

For the press-out, use a resistance band or cable that is placed on something sturdy and just above shoulder-height.

With your knuckles pointed up to the sky, press out horizontally.

Try not to go too far back with the shoulder, and make sure the hand stays in line with the moving elbow.

For the floor press, grab a dumbbell and lie on your back.

Make sure your knees are bent and that your back is fairly flat.

Press the weight up to the sky, then lower down under control.

Tom House 90/90's
Week 1: 5 Each / Week 2: 6 Each / Week 3: 7 Each / Week 4: 8 Each

Place the elbows at shoulder-height and at 90-degree angles.

Keep one arm back while lowering the other.

Do the prescribed amount from each of three positions: palms toward your ears; thumbs toward your ears; and then palms away from your ears.

STRENGTH – PHASE 1 (Circuit 1 – Day 2 & 4)

Perform in Order for 3 Rounds Each

Single Leg 5-Second Hip Lift Holds Off Bench
Week 1: 5 Reps / Week 2: 6 Reps / Week 3: 7 Reps / Week 4: 8 Reps

Start by lying back against a weight bench. The edge of the bench should line up just below your shoulder blades.

From there, place your knees at a 90-degree angle with your hands behind your head for support.

Bring one knee toward your chest and hold for five seconds, keeping the foot on the floor flat.

You should feel this in the back of the leg that's on the ground. If you feel this in the lower back, keep two feet on the ground and squeeze as if you're cracking a walnut between your glutes, to ensure that you are activating the right muscles.

Half-Kneeling Single Arm Row or Dumbbell Row with Pause
Week 1: 12 Each / Week 2-3: 10 Each / Week 4: 8 Each

Pick the exercise that suits your situation best.

For the band row, get in a half-kneeling position and place the band at about knee- to hip-height.

Grab the handle with the arm of the lead leg.

Pull the cable or band toward your chest, pause, and then control on the way back out.

Make sure the shoulder goes back with the elbow as you row in.

For the dumbbell row, lean into something sturdy like a bench or box.

Lean forward and keep the spine neutral.

From there, row the weight toward your chest, pause, then control on the way down.

Again, make sure the shoulder goes back with the elbow!

Half-Kneeling Lift
Week 1: 8 Each / Week 2- 3: 10 Each / Week 4: 12 Each

Attach the band to something sturdy and close to ground height.

Make sure the outside leg is up and the inside leg is kneeling on the ground.

Grip the band as if you were driving a motorcycle, and lift up. Make sure your arms move with your core, and that you stay straight as you lift upward.

Keep this movement under control and the lower body stable.

Brandon Gaydorus & Lauren McMillin

STRENGTH – PHASE 1 (Circuit 2 – Day 2 & 4)

Perform in Order for 3 Rounds Each

Stiff Leg Off Bench Hip Lift Holds
Week 1: 30 Sec. / Week 2: 35 Sec. / Week 3: 40 Sec. / Week 4: 45 Sec.

Place the bottom of your shoulder blades on the edge of a bench or box and straighten your body so that it is parallel with the floor.

Squeeze your butt as if you were cracking a walnut between it and feel like you are tensing your abdominal muscles to keep everything tight.

<u>Alternative: Stiff Leg Hip Lifts Off Ground</u>

Keep everything the same as the straight leg hip lift, but place the back of the shoulders on the ground.

Half-Kneeling Single Arm Vertical Pulldown
Week 1: 12 Each / Week 2-3: 10 Each / Week 4: 8 Each

Attach a band or cable at shoulder-height or higher. Pull down with the same arm as the kneeling leg and twist the knuckles away from your body.

Make sure that the shoulder goes back with elbow.

Eccentric Calf Raise
Week 1-2: 12 Reps / Week 3-4: 15 Reps

Lightly hold onto an object and place your toes on an elevated surface.

On the way down, bend your knees slightly to load the back of your calves. The eccentric motion for this exercise should take about three seconds.

Lift the heels up to repeat. This can be done with or without a weight as shown in the pictures.

WARM-UP CIRCUIT – PHASE 2 (Day 1 & 3)

Perform in Order for 2 Rounds Each

Front Plank

Place your forearms on the ground and elbows directly below the shoulders. Hold for 20 seconds.

If performed properly, this should feel like your elbows are sliding toward your feet, and that you are bracing as if about to take a punch to the stomach.

Single Leg Hip Lifts

Lying on your back, dig one heel into the ground and drive the opposing knee toward the chest.

Tuck the hips and lift up to form a straight line from your shoulders to the knee of the foot on the ground.

Hold for a brief second at the top, then lift down with control. Perform 8 times, then repeat with the other leg.

If you feel tension in your lower back, resort to the hip lift with two feet on the ground as shown in the second picture.

Bird Dogs

From a quadruped position, place your hands directly under your shoulders and start with your knees at about a 90-degree angle, as pictured below.

Extend one arm forward and the opposite leg back, parallel to the floor. Hold for five seconds with the ankle flexed toward the shin.

After that, bring the elbow and opposing knee toward each other.

Perform 5 times, then repeat on the other side.

Progression: Bird Dogs with Mini-Band

If you want a little bit more of a challenge on this exercise, place a light mini-band around the middle of the feet as pictured below.

Standing Chest Press

Place a resistance band on something sturdy at about shoulder-height.

Start from a golf stance. Extend the hips forward as you press the band out. Perform 8 times.

Your first couple of reps shouldn't be too fast, but you can gradually increase the tempo to make the movement as explosive as possible.

Assisted Band Jumps

Attach a resistance band to something sturdy above the height of your head.

Load like you normally would for a jump, except hold onto the band instead of placing your hands behind your back.

Explode up. Try aiming for about a 10-20 percent increase on your vertical jump with the resistance. Try not to make the resistance too strong. Perform 5 times.

Alternative: Single Leg Deceleration Jumps

If you don't want to jump, or are unable to perform the assisted band jumps, try single leg deceleration jumps instead.

Start by raising your hands overhead and lifting up onto your toes.

Then drop down onto one leg and whip that same hand back behind you as quick as possible.

Stick the landing under control. Perform 5 times, then repeat with the other leg.

WARM-UP CIRCUIT – PHASE 2 (Day 2 & 4)

Perform in Order for 2 Rounds Each

Side Plank

Place your elbow directly below your shoulder. Keep your feet together, or place the top foot in front of the back, whichever feels better to you.

From there, press your elbow and feet into the ground and lift up. Hold for a brief second. Perform 8 times, then repeat on the other side of your body.

A good place to put the top hand is on the hip.

Lateral Lunge with Step Out

Start with your feet together before stepping out into a wide stance.

Sink into that same hip and straighten the opposite leg. Perform 5 times, then repeat with the other leg.

Focus more on loading the glute than the depth of the lunge.

It should feel like you're sitting back when performing this movement correctly. You can reach your hands out to help counterbalance the movement.

Single Leg Balance with Torso Rotation

Get into a golf posture and shift all your weight onto one leg.

Keep the lower body still and rotate the upper body from side to side, just like in the golf swing. Perform 8 times, then repeat with the other leg.

Split Stance Rotational Band Throws

Make sure the band is attached to something sturdy, and interlock your fingers for a firm grip.

Act as if you're throwing a ball over your lead leg. Control the movement of the band as you go.

Perform 8 times, then switch to the other leg. Gradually increase the speed throughout the exercise.

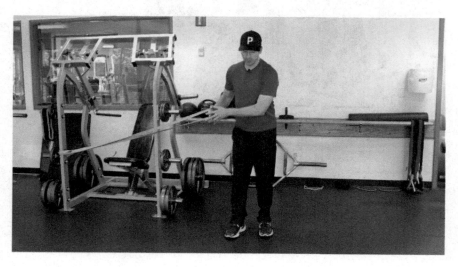

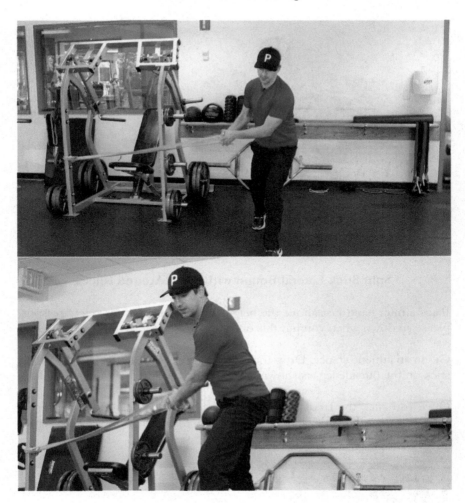

Split Stick Lateral Bound with Band Around Knees

Place a mini-band just above the height of your knees. (For safety reasons, please sit down when you put this on.)

Get in an athletic stance. Drop the inside foot back, then quickly switch to a stick on the outside leg, as shown in the fourth picture.

Once you stick the landing and are balanced on the outside foot, laterally bound to the other side, and stick the landing. Perform 5 times, then repeat with the other leg.

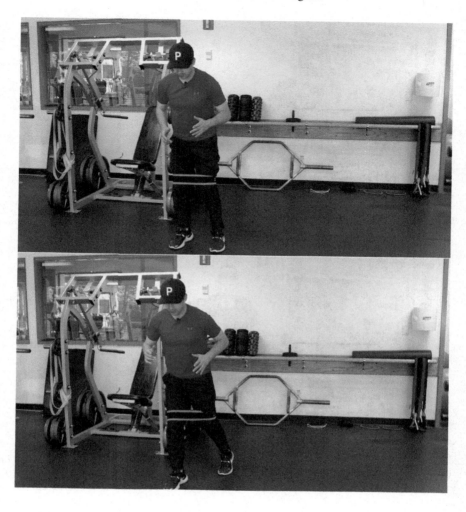

STRENGTH – PHASE 2 (Circuit 1 – Day 1 & 3)

Perform in Order for 3 Rounds Each

Rear Foot Elevated Oscillating Split Squat
Week 1-4: 8 Reps Each Side

Place one foot on an elevated surface such as a bench or box.

On the way down, keep a straight line from your back knee to your head. You should be leaning forward slightly, and the front shin angle should be close to parallel, with the spine angle at the bottom position.

For the oscillating part of this exercise, go all the way down, then halfway up, then back down for the prescribed amount of reps.

Make sure the front foot stays flat and that you do this exercise fairly quickly. You can do this with or without dumbbells.

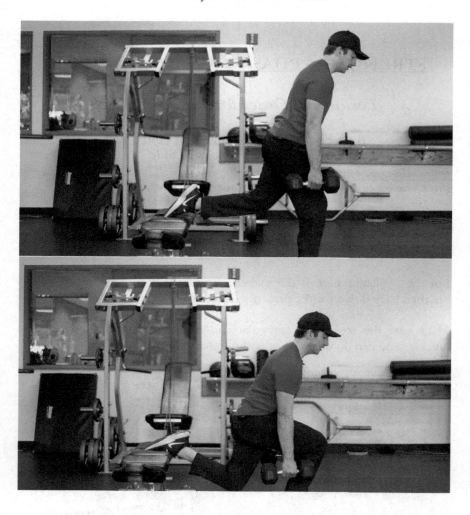

<u>Alternative: Oscillating Split Squat</u>

If elevating the back foot is too challenging or uncomfortable, perform this exercise with your back foot on the ground as pictured below.

Incline Bench or Iso-Split Stance Overhead Band Press
Week 1-4: 8 Reps Each Side

Pick which exercise fits you best.

For the incline bench, place the dumbbells on your thighs and keep them close to your chest as you fall backwards.

Then press the dumbbells up and down under control.

For the split stance single arm press, push up at about a 45-60 degree angle with the opposite hand of the lead leg.

Control the movement on the way down. Repeat for the prescribed number of reps before switching sides.

Standing Chops
Week 1: 8 Reps / Week 2-3: 10 Reps / Week 4: 12 Reps

From a golf stance, attach a band above head-height.

Grip the band as if you were riding a motorcycle.

Keep your arms straight and chop the band down toward the lead hip.

Control on the way up. Repeat for the prescribed amount.

STRENGTH – PHASE 2 (Circuit 2 – Day 1 & 3)

Perform in Order for 3 Rounds Each

Partial Squat
Week 1-4: 8 Reps Each Side

From a split stance, place your back toes in line with the lead heel as shown below.

Maintain most of your weight on the lead foot, with the back heel lifted off the ground. Lower to the bottom position of a jump before exploding up.

If you jump off the ground, it is a sign that you need more weight.

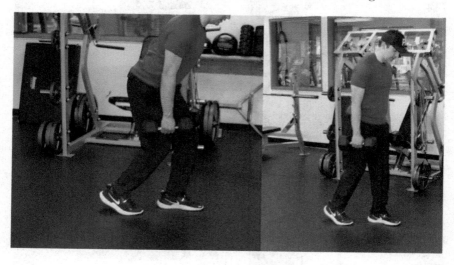

Single Arm Eccentric Press-Outs
Week 1-4: 8 Reps Each Side

Attach a band to something sturdy around shoulder-height, and get into a split stance.

Press the band out with the same hand as the back leg, at a normal tempo, and take three seconds as you bring it back in under control.

Most of the weight will be on the lead foot, but you will need to push off the back toes to get the most out of this exercise.

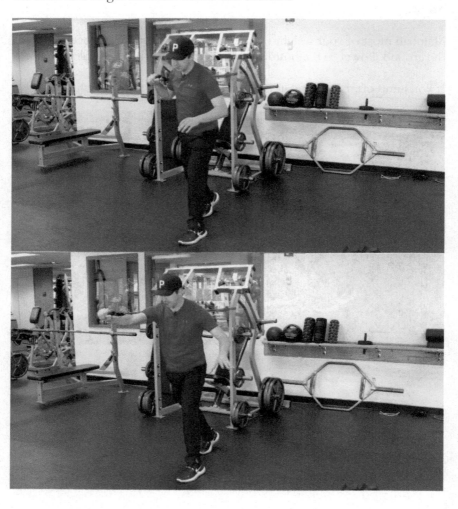

Tom House Push-Pulls
Week 1-2: 10 Seconds Each / Week 3-4: 15 Seconds Each

Place your forearms parallel to the floor and pull your hands apart. After timing for the prescribed amount, reverse the grip.

For the pushes, do the same movement except press the palms of the hands together as pictured. Only perform the pushes once.

In the pulls, you should feel activation in the back of the shoulders. With the pushes, you should feel tension on the front part of the chest.

185

STRENGTH – PHASE 2 (Circuit 1 - Day 2 & 4)

Perform in Order for 3 Rounds Each

Eccentric Romanian Deadlifts (RDL) with Dumbbell or Band
Week 1-4: 8 Reps

Place your feet about shoulder-width apart, and let the dumbbells slide down the front of your legs as you take three seconds to lower them.

Maintain a slight bend in the knees. It should feel like your butt is going back and a little bit up as you lower the dumbbells.

As you transition to an upwards movement, make sure to keep your core tight and sturdy. If you feel pain in your lower back during this exercise, please reach out to a trainer or medical professional for advice.

If you choose to do this with the band, everything remains the same, but place the band around the middle of your feet and grip it at the sides of your legs.

Split Stance Single Arm Eccentric Row or Dumbbell Row
Week 1-4: 8 Reps

Pick which exercise fits your situation best.

For the split stance row, attach the band to something sturdy or use a cable cross machine. The attachment should be about chest height.

Get into a split stance and row inward with the same arm as the lead foot. From there, go back slowly for about three seconds as you release tension to the starting position.

If you choose the eccentric dumbbell row, make sure to maintain a neutral spine, and lean against a sturdy object such as a bench.

Pull your shoulder back with your elbow, and lower the dumbbell slowly for about three seconds.

Standing Lift
Week 1: 8 Reps / Week 2-3: 10 Reps / Week 4: 12 Reps

From a golf stance, attach a band low to a sturdy object and grip it as though driving a motorcycle.

Lift up to about shoulder-height. Make sure you're doing this movement with your core, not just your arms. You can also perform this on a cable cross machine instead of using a band.

STRENGTH – PHASE 2 (Circuit 2 – Day 2 & 4)

Perform in Order for 3 Rounds Each

Alternating Stiff Leg Hip Lift
Week 1-4: 8 Reps

Lie on your back and keep a slight bend in your knees.

Flex your ankles toward you and dig your heels into the ground.

Lift one foot just barely off the ground before alternating to the other side.

Two Arm Vertical Pulldown
Week 1: 12 Reps / Week 2-3: 10 Reps / Week 4: 8 Reps

Attach a band at about head-height or even slightly higher.

Hold the handles and get into a half-kneeling position.

Pull the band toward your chest. Make sure the elbows go back with the shoulders and that you control the movement on the way back up.

Try to move the shoulders as smoothly as possible throughout this exercise.

Single Leg Eccentric Calf Raise
Week 1-2: 12 Reps / Week 3-4: 15 Reps

This exercise can be performed with or without a weight, but make sure to lightly hold onto something as shown in the picture.

Start by placing the front part of your foot on a slightly elevated object and rising up on the balls of your feet.

Take three seconds to lower, so that your foot is parallel to the floor. Keep a slight bend in the knee while doing so.

The point of this exercise is to load and activate the calf, so check that you're feeling that while replicating the positions in the pictures.

WARM-UP CIRCUIT – PHASE 3 (Day 1 & 3)

Perform in Order for 2 Rounds Each

Long Lever Plank
Week 1-4: 20-Second Hold

Place your elbows slightly past your shoulders as pictured below.

Act as if you're cracking a walnut between your glutes to create tension. If you feel this in your lower back, revert back to a normal front plank.

Single Leg Bucks
Week 1-4: 8 Reps Each Side

Place the edge of your foot on a box, bench or other sturdy object, about one to two feet off the ground.

Straighten the other leg toward the sky and push the opposite foot into the box before lifting the hips.

On the upward movement, make the top foot reach toward the sky, and then control it on the way down.

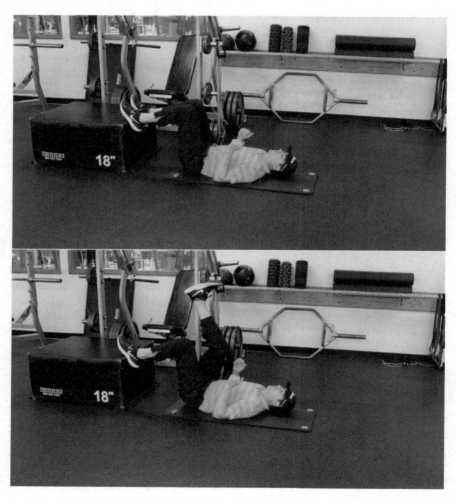

Standing Bird Dogs
Week 1-4: 8 Reps Each Side

Bring one knee up so that the thigh is parallel with the floor. Keep the bottom leg straight the entire time.

Reach your hands up and down for the prescribed amount of reps.

To make this more challenging, use a weighted object like a ViPR PRO or a golf club, as shown in the pictures.

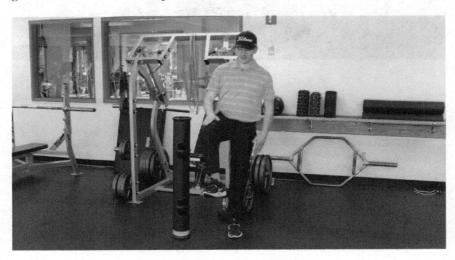

Sprinter Chest Press
Week 1-4: 5 Reps Each Side

Place the bands on something sturdy a little higher than the height of your shoulders and grab a side with each hand.

Step out and press out rapidly, controlling on the way in.

Split Stance Dumbbell Jumps
Week 1-4: 3 Jumps Each Side

Grab two fairly light dumbbells and get into a split stance, with the front toes and back heel off the ground.

Shift forward onto the lead foot and stomp the front toes down.

Let the back foot catch up and load along with the lead foot, before exploding upward. Land softly and repeat for the prescribed amount of reps. This can be performed with or without dumbbells.

<u>Alternative: Single Leg Deceleration Jumps</u>
Week 1-4: 5 Each Side

If you can't do the assisted band jumps, do single leg deceleration jumps.

Start by raising your hands up to the sky and lift up on your toes.

Then drop down onto one leg and whip that same hand back behind you as quickly as possible.

Stick the landing under control and repeat.

WARM-UP CIRCUIT – PHASE 3 (Day 2 & 4)

Perform in Order for 2 Rounds Each

Side Plank with Adduction
Week 1-4: 5 (5 Second) Holds Each Side

Place your feet on top of each other, or staggered with the top foot in front. Make sure the shoulder is directly above the elbow.

Press your feet and forearm into the ground and lift the hips.

Then lift the top leg while keeping the foot parallel with the floor.

Hold for five seconds and repeat 5 times, then repeat with other leg. You should feel this exercise mostly on the outside of the top hip.

Lateral Lunge + Side Shuffle
Week 1-4: 5 Each Way

Lunge into the outside leg and take three shuffles to the side, before lunging to the other side.

When you lunge, reach the opposite hand toward the foot as pictured below.

Single Leg Helicopter Twists
Week 1: 5 Each Side / Week 2: 6 Ea. / Week 3: 7 Ea. / Week 4: 8 Ea.

Get into a golf stance and balance on one leg.

Place your hands out to the side.

Do your best to maintain the full outstretch of your arms. Keep your lower body fairly still as you twist to each side.

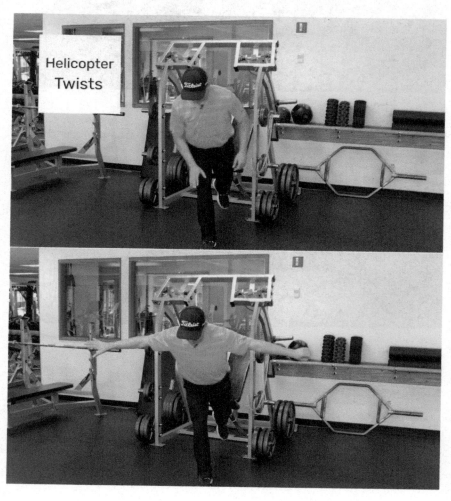

Rotational Band Throw
Week 1-4: 8 Each Side

Attach a band to something sturdy at about waist-height.

Load and explode the resistance forward, as if throwing a medicine ball as far as possible.

Control on the way back in and repeat 8 times, then repeat on the other side.

Make sure to start slow and increase the speed as you go.

Lateral Bound to a Sprint
Week 1-4: 3 Each Side

From a seated position, laterally bound to the opposite side from which you pushed off.

Stick the landing, then sprint forward for about 10 yards. Perform 3 times, then repeat with the other leg.

STRENGTH – PHASE 3 (Circuit 1 – Day 1 & 3)

Perform in Order for the Prescribed Amount

Week 1: 3 Rounds
Week 2: 4 Rounds
Week 3: 4 Rounds
Week 4: 5 Rounds

Goblet Squat with Pause + Explosion
Week 1: 8 Reps / Week 2-3: 6 Reps / Week 4: 5 Reps

Grab a weighted object, preferably a kettlebell or dumbbell. Shoot for about 60 percent of your max squat weight.

Keeping it close to your chest, squat down so that your thighs are about parallel to the floor, pause for a brief second, and then explode up. A bench can help you determine how low to squat.

Split Stance Overhead Press or Incline Bench Press
Week 1: 8 Reps / Week 2-3: 6 Reps / Week 4: 5 Reps

Pick which exercise fits you best.

For the split stance single arm press, push up the band or cable at about a 45-60 degree angle with the opposite hand of the lead leg.

Control the movement on the way down. Repeat for the prescribed amount of reps before switching sides.

For the incline bench, place the dumbbells on your thighs and keep them close to your chest as you fall backwards.

Then press the dumbbells up and down under a controlled and smooth movement.

Speed Chops
Week 1: 8 Reps / Week 2-3: 10 Reps / Week 4: 12 Reps

From a golf stance, attach a band above head-height. Grip the band as if you were riding a motorcycle.

Keep your arms straight and chop the band down toward the lead hip at a rapid pace.

Start slow and pick up speed as you go. Control the movement on the way up and repeat for the prescribed amount.

STRENGTH – PHASE 3 (Circuit 2 – Day 1 & 3)

Perform in Order for the Prescribed Amount

Week 1: 3 Rounds
Week 2: 4 Rounds
Week 3: 4 Rounds
Week 4: 5 Rounds

Rear Foot Elevated Split Squat with Dumbbells or Body Weight
Week 1-4: 6 Reps Each Side

Place your knee on something comfortable and elevate your foot onto an object about 12-18 inches off the ground. Lift the front foot just barely off the ground, before pressing it back into the ground and exploding up.

Typically, dumbbells between 15-25 pounds work well for this exercise. If you find yourself jumping while doing this exercise, then add weight. If you are going up too slowly, then decrease weight.

If this position bothers your back knee, avoid elevating the back foot, as shown below.

Split Stance Press-Out
Week 1: 8 Reps / Week 2-3: 6 Reps / Week 4: 5 Reps

From a split stance, keep a slight bend in the lead leg and lift the back heel off the ground.

The attachment should be about the height of your shoulder. Press out the band or cable horizontally with the same arm as the back foot.

Control as you move back to the starting position. Maintain a smooth shoulder movement throughout the exercise.

<u>Tom House Arm Circles</u>
Week 1-4: 10 Seconds Each Position or Until 90% Fatigue

Place your shoulders back, with your elbows slightly bent.

Perform smooth and controlled arm circles forward and backward for the prescribed amount, first in small circles, then medium, then large.

Change your hand position in each round, from palms up to thumbs up, then palms down, to hit the shoulder a little bit differently each time.

STRENGTH – PHASE 3 (Circuit 1 – Day 2 & 4)

Perform in Order for the Prescribed Amount

Week 1: 3 Rounds
Week 2: 4 Rounds
Week 3: 4 Rounds
Week 4: 5 Rounds

Dumbbell or Band Romanian Deadlift (RDL)
Week 1: 8 Reps / Week 2-3: 6 Reps / Week 4: 5 Reps

Choose which option fits your gym situation best, preferably with dumbbells if available.

Place the dumbbells in front of your thighs. Avoid slouching your shoulders.

Maintain a slight bend in your knees as you lower, bending mostly from the hips.

There should be a straight line from your hips to your neck at the bottom position, and you should feel this in the back of your legs.

For the banded version, place the band under the middle of your feet and grip on the sides. Feet should be about shoulder-width.

Make sure to maintain a neutral spine throughout the entire exercise.

Dumbbell Row or Split Stance Row
Week 1: 8 Reps / Week 2-3: 6 Reps / Week 4: 5 Reps (Each Side)

If you choose the dumbbell row, maintain a neutral spine and lean over on something sturdy, such as a bench.

Pull your shoulder back with your elbow, and lower the dumbbell under control.

For the split stance band row, attach the band to something sturdy or use a cable cross machine. The attachment should be about chest- to shoulder-height.

Get into a split stance and row inward with the same arm as the lead foot.

Control the movement back to the starting position.

Standing Lift with Speed
Week 1: 8 Reps / Week 2-3: 10 Reps / Week 4: 12 Reps (Each Side)

From a golf stance, attach a band or lower the cable to the height shown in the pictures. Grip the attachment as if you were driving a motorcycle as shown in the pictures.

Lift the band to about shoulder-height. Generate this movement from your core. Begin slow, and increase your speed as you go.

STRENGTH – PHASE 3 (CIRCUIT 2 – Day 2 & 4)

Perform in Order for the Prescribed Amount

Week 1: 3 Rounds
Week 2: 4 Rounds
Week 3: 4 Rounds
Week 4: 5 Rounds

Elevated Single Leg Resisted Hip Lift or Glute Bridge Walkout
Week 1: 8 Reps / Week 2-3: 6 Reps / Week 4: 5 Reps (Each Side)

For the elevated single leg resisted hip lift, find two objects about three feet apart that have similar height, like a bench and a box. Attach resistance bands to something sturdy, so that they sit stretched across your waist.

The base of your shoulder blades will rest on the edge of one box, with your feet on the other. Drive your opposite knee toward your chest as you lift and extend the hips.

If this exercise is too difficult to perform or set up, perform a glute bridge walkout instead.

For the glute bridge walkout, start by lying on your back and digging your heels into the ground.

With your ankles flexed, walk your legs out as far as you can without feeling pressure in your lower back.

The end range position is different for everyone, so the key is to feel it in your glutes and hamstrings the entire time.

Walk your feet in and out 5 times.

Two Arm Speed Pulldown
Week 1 – 12 Reps / Week 2-3: 10 Reps / Week 4: 8 Reps

Attach a fairly strong resistance band to something sturdy at an elevated height, above the head if possible. You can also use a cable cross machine.

Make sure the shoulders go back with the elbows as you pull down, and that you start slow before picking up speed along the way.

Always control the movement on the way up.

<u>Single Leg Explosive Calf Raise</u>
Week 1-2: 12 Reps Each Side / Week 3-4: 15 Reps Each Side

Elevated the ball of one foot onto an object about 2-8 inches off the ground.

To start, slightly bend the knee of the foot on the object to load the calf.

Drive the opposite foot back before then driving it up as quickly as you can. The heel will lift as the knee extends upward.

Do your best to follow the sequence in the pictures below. It is important to note that the elevated stationary foot should be parallel to the floor at the bottom position.

Perform In Order Listed (1 Round Through Each)

Phase 1 – Mobility

Hamstring Floss - 8 Each Side

Supine Hip External Rotations - 15 Sec. Each Side

Supine Side-to-Sides - 8 Each Side

Supine Pelvic Tilts - 8 Each

Side-Lying Open Books - 8 Each Side

Half-Kneeling Quad Pull w/Overhead Reach (Alt: Childs Pose) - 15 Sec. Each Side

Phase 2 – Mobility

Assisted Leg Lowers - 5 Each Side

90/90 Hip Internal + External Rotation - 5 Each Side

Half-Kneeling Adductor Walkout - 5 Each Side

Cat & Camel - 5 Each

Quadruped T-Spine Ext. Rotations - 5 Each Side

Seated Lateral Tilts or Tall-Kneeling Lateral Flexion - 5 Each Side

Phase 3 – Mobility

Toe Touches (Toes Up + Heels Up) - 5 Each

Standing Twists (*Hold on to something) - 8 Each Side

Leg Swings - 15 Each Side

Pelvic Tilts - 8 Each

Torso Rotations - 8 Each Side

Lateral Line Stretch - 15 Sec. Each Side

Perform Each Exercise in a Circuit for a total of 3 rounds

Phase 1 – Stability (Day 1 & 3)

Glute Bridge Holds - 30 Sec.

Iso-Split Squat Hold with Twist (Alt: Half Kneeling) - 8 Each

Side-Lying Abductions (10-Sec. Hold) - 2 Each Side

Plank from Hands and Knees - 8 Deep Breaths

Half-Kneeling Golf Club Chop/Lift - 8 Each Side

Side Plank 5-Sec. Hold from Knees (Alt: Star Plank - 25 Sec. Ea.) - 5 Each Side

Phase 1 – Stability (Day 2 & 4)

Full Ankle Dorsiflexion Split Squat - 8 Each

Single Leg Balance - 15 Sec.

Glute Max Press-Out (5-Sec. Holds) - 5 Each Side

Supine Hip Drops - 8 Each Side

Tall-Kneeling Golf Swings - 3 Each Side

90/90 Isometric Holds - 10 Sec. Each Position

Perform Each Exercise in a Circuit for a total of 3 rounds

Phase 2 – Stability (Day 1 & 3)

Single Leg Glute Bridge Holds (10-Sec. Hold) - 3 Each Side

Quarter Squat with Rotation - 8 Each Side

Side-Lying Adduction Off Bench (2-Sec. Hold) - 8 Each Side

Plank - 8 Deep Breaths

Split Stance Chop/Lift - 8 Each Side

Side Plank from Knees with Abduction (Alt: Star Plank - 25 Sec. Ea.) - 5 Each Side

Phase 2 – Stability (Day 2 & 4)

Split Squat (5-Sec. Holds) - 5 Each

Single Leg Balance with Alternating Reach - 8 Each Side

Glute Max Mini-Band Circuit (10-Sec. Hold at the End) - 8 Each Side

Supine Dead Bug with Golf Club - 6 Each Side

Standing Swings - 5 Each Side

Tom House Push-Pulls - 15 Sec. Each

Perform Each Exercise in a Circuit for a total of 3 rounds

Phase 3 – Stability (Day 1 & 3)

Single Leg Glute Bridge - 8 Each

Iso-Single Leg Deadlift with Twists - 5 Each Side

Side-Lying Adduction Off Bench with Lift (5-Sec. Hold) - 3 Each Side

Shoulder Taps - 5 Each Side

Lateral Lunge with Twist - 5 Each Side

Side Plank (Alt: Star Plank - 25 Sec. Ea.) - 8 Each Side

Phase 3 – Stability (Day 2 & 4)

Single Leg Split Squat - 8 Each Side

Single Leg Balance with Rotation - 8 Each Side

Stiff Leg Lateral Walks - 8 Each Side

Extended Dead Bugs - 6 Each Side

Stepping Swings - 5 Each Side

Tom House Arm Circles - 10 Sec. Each

*NJP - Represents *No Jumping Protocol*, if you don't feel comfortable jumping or have pain when doing so, please do the NJP exercise instead.

*RE - Represents **an alternative exercise** if the one listed doesn't feel quite right.

Phase 1 – Warm-Up Circuit: Day 1 & 3

Perform in a circuit for a total of 2 Rounds Each

Push-Up Hold or Plank from Hands & Knees - Hold for 8 breaths

Single Leg Hip Lift (10-Sec. Holds) (RE: Hip Lift) - 3 Each Side

Dead Bugs w/Golf Club - 8 Each Side

TK Band Chest Press-Out - 8 Ea.

Deceleration Jumps + Jump Squats (NJP: Deceleration Jumps) - 5 Ea.

Phase 1 – Workout: Day 1 & 3

Perform in a circuit for a total of 3 Rounds Each

Circuit 1:

Oscillating Squat (*Can use any type of weight or do bodyweight) - 12 Reps

Half-Kneeling Single Arm Overhead Band Press or Single Arm Slight Incline DB Bench Press – Week 1 (12 Ea.), Week 2 & 3 (10 Ea.), Week 4 (8 Ea.)

Half-Kneeling Chop – Week 1 (8 Ea.), Week 2 & 3 (10 Ea.), Week 4 (8 Ea.)

Circuit 2:

2 DB's RFE (5-Sec. Hold) + Explode (RE: Split Squat Holds) - 5 Each Side

Half-Kneeling Single Arm Band Press – Week 1 (12 Ea.), Week 2 & 3 (10 Ea.), Week 4 (8 Ea.)

Tom House Alternating Shoulder 90/90's (RE: 10-Sec. Iso-Metric Holds) – Week 1 (5 Ea.), Week 2 (6 Ea.), Week 3 (7 Ea.), Week 4 (8 Ea.)

Phase 1 – Warm-Up Circuit: Day 2 & 4

Perform in a circuit for a total of 2 Rounds through

Side Plank from Knees with Abduction (5-Sec. Hold) - 5 Each Side

Alternating Lateral Lunge - 5 Each Side

Single Leg Balance - 15 Sec. Each Side

Half-Kneeling Rotational Band Throw - 8 Each Side

Lateral Bound with Stick (NJP: Alternating Single Leg Balance – 15 Sec. Holds) - 5 Each Side

Phase 1 – Workout: Day 2 & 4

Perform in a circuit for a total of 3 Rounds through

Circuit 1:

Single-Leg Off Bench Hip Lift (5 Sec. Holds) – Week 1 (5 Ea.), Week 2 (6 Ea.), Week 3 (7 Ea.), Week 4 (8 Ea.)

Half-Kneeling Single Arm Row with Pause or DB Row with Pause – Week 1 (12 Ea.), Week 2 & 3 (10 Ea.), Week 4 (8 Ea.)

Half-Kneeling Lift – Week 1 (8 Ea.), Week 2 & 3 (10 Ea.), Week 4 (12 Ea.)

Circuit 2:

Reverse Plank or Straight Leg Plank – Week 1 (30 Sec.), Week 2 (35 Sec.), Week 3 (40 Sec.), Week 4 (45 Sec.)

Half-Kneeling Single-Arm Vertical Pulldown – Week 1 (12 Ea.), Week 2 & 3 (10 Ea.), Week 4 (8 Ea.)

Eccentric Calf Raise – Week 1 & 2 (12 Reps), Week 3 & 4 (15 Reps)

Phase 2 – Warm-Up Circuit: Day 1 & 3

Perform in a circuit for a total of 2 Rounds through

Front Plank - Hold for 8 breaths

Single Leg Hip Lift (RE: Hip Lift) - 8 Each Side

Bird Dogs (5-Sec. Holds) - 5 Each Side

Standing Band Chest Press Pass - 8 Reps

Band Assisted Jumps (NJP: Single Leg Deceleration Jumps - 5 Ea.) - 8 Jumps

Phase 2 – Workout: Day 1 & 3

Perform in a circuit for a total of 3 Rounds through

Circuit 1:

Rear Foot Elevated Oscillating Split Squat (RE: Perform without weight) – 8 Each Side

Iso-Single Arm Overhead Band Press or Low Incline DB Bench Press – 8 Each Side

Standing Chops – Week 1 (8 Ea.), Week 2 & 3 (10 Ea.), Week 4 (12 Ea.)

Circuit 2:

Partial Squats - 8 Each Side

Eccentric Split Stance Band Press Out - 8 Each Side

Tom House Push-Pulls – Week 1 & 2 (10 Sec. Ea.), Week 3 & 4 (15 Sec. Ea.)

Phase 2 – Warm-Up Circuit: Day 2 & 4

Perform in a circuit for a total of 2 Rounds through

Side Plank - 8 Each Side

Lateral Lunge with Step Out - 5 Each Side

Single Leg Balance with Torso Rotation - 8 Each Side

Split Stance Rotational Throw with Band - 8 Each Side

Split Switch Lateral Bound with Stick (NJP: No Bound) - 5 Each Side

Phase 2 – Workout: Day 2 & 4

Perform in a circuit for a total of 3 Rounds through

Circuit 1:

Eccentric Romanian Deadlift with Dumbbells or Band - 8 Reps

Eccentric Split Stance Single Arm Row or Dumbbell Eccentric Row - 8 Each Side

Standing Lift – Week 1 (8 Ea.), Week 2 & 3 (10 Ea.), Week 4 (12 Ea.)

Circuit 2:

Alternating Stiff Leg Hip Lift - 8 Each Side

Half-Kneeling Two-Arm Vertical Pulldown – Week 1 (12 Reps), Week 2 & 3 (10 Reps), Week 4 (8 Reps)

SL Eccentric Calf Raise – Week 1 & 2 (12 Reps), Week 3 & 4 (15 Reps)

Phase 3 – Warm-Up Circuit: Day 1 & 3

Perform in a circuit for a total of 2 Rounds through

Long Lever Plank – Hold for 20 Seconds

Single Leg Bucks - 8 Each Side

Standing Bird Dogs - 8 Each Side

Stepping Sprinter Chest Press Pass - 5 Each Side

Two Dumbbell Split Stance Jumps (*Can do without the weight if no dumbbells) (NJP: Stepping Deceleration Jumps – 5 Ea.) - 3 Each Side

Phase 3 – Workout: Day 1 & 3

Perform in a circuit for a total of
(Week 1 – 3 Rounds, Week 2 & 3 – 4 Rounds, Week 4 – 5 Rounds)

Circuit 1:

Goblet Squat to Box with Pause + Explosion – Week 1 (8 Reps), Week 2 & 3 (6 Reps), Week 4 (5 Reps)

Single Arm Band Overhead Press or Low Incline Dumbbell Bench Press – Week 1 (8 Reps), Week 2-3 (6 Reps), Week 4 (5 Reps)

Speed Chops – Week 1 (8 Ea.), Week 2 & 3 (10 Ea.), Week 4 (12 Ea.)

Circuit 2:

Split Squats with Lift Off - 6 Each Side

Split Stance Band Press Out – Week 1 (8 Ea.), Week 2 & 3 (10 Ea.), Week 4 (5 Ea.)

Tom House Arm Circles - 10 Seconds Each Position or Until 90% Fatigue

Phase 3 – Warm-Up Circuit: Day 2 & 4

Perform in a circuit for a total of 2 Rounds through

Side Plank (5-Sec. Holds) or Side Planks with Abduction - 5 Each Side

Lateral Lunge + Side Shuffle - 5 Each Side

Single Leg Helicopter Twists - 8 Each Side

Standing Rotational Throw with Band - 8 Each Side

Lateral Bound + Sprint (*NJP - Stepping Deceleration Jumps) – 3 Each Side

Phase 3 – Workout: Day 2 & 4

Perform in a circuit for a total of
(Week 1 – 3 Rounds, Week 2 & 3 – 4 Rounds, Week 4 – 5 Rounds)

Circuit 1:

Dumbbell or Band Romanian Deadlift (RDL) – Week 1 (8 Reps), Week 2 & 3 (6 Reps), Week 4 (5 Reps)

Split Stance Single Arm Row or Dumbbell Row – Week 1 (8 Ea.), Week (6 Ea.), Week 4 (5 Ea.)

Standing Lifts with Speed – Week 1 (8 Ea.), Week 2-3 (10 Ea.), Week 4 (12 Ea.)

Circuit 2:

Elevated Single Leg Resisted Hip Lift (RE: Glute Bridge Walkout - 5 Ea.) – Week 1 (8 Ea.), Week 2 & 3 (6 Ea.), Week 4 (5 Ea.)

Two Arm Speed Pulldown – Week 1 (12 Reps), Week 2 & 3 (10 Reps), Week 4 (8 Reps)

SL Functional Calf Raise – Week 1 & 2 (12 Ea.), Week 3 & 4 (15 Ea.)

ABOUT THE AUTHORS

Brandon Gaydorus

Brandon was recognized in 2019 as one of Golf Digest's Top 50 Golf Fitness Trainers in America. He is also the author of *The Ultimate In-Home Golf Fitness Program* which has sold over a thousand copies worldwide. In 2020, *Golf Digest* writer Joel Beall used Brandon as his trainer for *The Bryson Experiment*, where he had an average increase of 10 yards with his driver through 12 weeks of training.

Lauren McMillin

Lauren is the founder of YoGolf Performance. She is a 200-hour Registered Yoga Teacher, certified Katherine Roberts' Human Performance for Athletes Instructor, Yoga for Golfers Level 2 Instructor, Yoga for Seniors Instructor, Nationally Certified Pilates Teacher, Certified TPI Expert, and a member of the National Association of Certified Yoga Teachers.

With extensive training in Chain Reaction Biomechanics, Lauren's focus is to help athletes cultivate integrated joint and muscle stabilization, improve mobility, achieve greater range of motion, and learn sport-specific kinematic sequencing, to feel better and perform their best regardless of age, experience or injury.

Together, McMillin and Gaydorus teamed up to co-produce two seasons of Golf Mobility Pro, a YouTube series to help golfers move well and play better golf all over the world.

Made in the USA
Columbia, SC
24 September 2024

42262704R00153